The Impact of Science and Technology

HEALTH AND MEDICINE

Anne Rooney

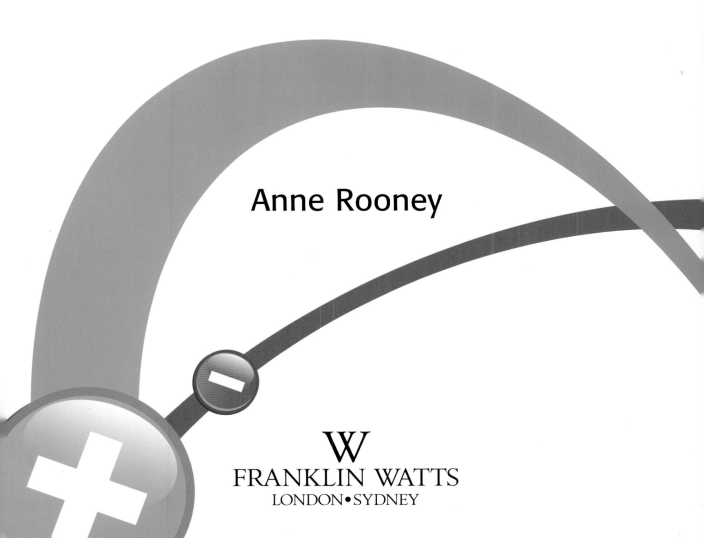

W
FRANKLIN WATTS
LONDON•SYDNEY

First published in 2009 by Franklin Watts

Copyright © 2009 Arcturus Publishing Limited

Franklin Watts
338 Euston Road
London NW1 3BH

Franklin Watts Australia
Level 17/207 Kent Street
Sydney, NSW 2000

Produced by Arcturus Publishing Limited
26/27 Bickels Yard
151-153 Bermondsey Street
London SE1 3HA

Series concept: Alex Woolf
Editor and picture researcher: Nicola Barber
Cover design and illustration: Phipps Design
Consultant: Mike Kent

A CIP catalogue record for this book is available
from the British Library.

Dewey Decimal Classification Number: 610

ISBN 978 0 7496 9222 3

Printed in China

Franklin Watts is a division of Hachette
Children's Books, an Hachette UK company.
www.hachette.co.uk

Picture credits
Corbis: 4, 22, 38 (Bettmann), 10 (Stapleton Collection),
15 (Chen Xiaowei/Xinhua Press), 24 (Franco Tanel/epa),
43 (CHU Amiens/epa), 44 (Jim Craigmyle),
46 (Wolfgang Langenstrassen/dpa), 48 (Pallava Bagla).
Science Photo Library: cover (David Mack), 7, 58 (Peter Menzel),
8, 36 (Antonia Reeve), 12 (Dr P. Marazzi), 17 (CDC),
18 (Steve Gschmeissner), 27 (Andrew Leonard),
29 (Pascal Goetgheluck), 30 (Volker Steger), 40 (Philippe Plailly),
56 (Coneyl Jay).
Shutterstock: 16 (Sebastian Kaulitzki), 20 (Leah-Anne Thompson),
21 (Alena Yar), 33 (Carolina K. Smith, M.D.), 34 (Simon Pedersen),
50 (Michael Taylor), 53 (Aaron Amat), 54 (AGphotographer).

Cover picture: computer artwork illustrates in vitro fertilization
(IVF), showing human egg cells in test tubes.

Every attempt has been made to clear copyright. Should there
be any inadvertent omission, please apply to the publisher for
rectification.

CONTENTS

CHAPTER 1
Science and Medicine   4

CHAPTER 2
High-Tech Hospitals   6

CHAPTER 3
Superhumans   12

CHAPTER 4
Fighting Disease   16

CHAPTER 5
Genetics   26

CHAPTER 6
Looking inside the Body   32

CHAPTER 7
Organ Transplants   38

CHAPTER 8
Public and Private Health   44

CHAPTER 9
Changing Lifestyles   50

CHAPTER 10
Meeting New Challenges   58

Glossary   60
Further Information   63
Index   64

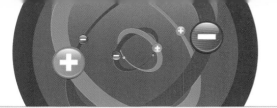

Science and Medicine

Developments in science and technology have been quickly adopted by medical science. New discoveries in subjects ranging from space exploration to robotics are often applied to medicine, helping doctors both to prolong life and improve its quality.

Early progress

The foundations of modern-day medicine were laid hundreds of years ago. The development of magnifying lenses led to the invention of the microscope in around 1590. For the first time, scientists could see that there are tiny living things – microorganisms – swarming all around us, and that our own bodies are made up of cells of different types. In 1865,

In 1869, Joseph Lister began using a spray of carbolic acid to kill germs during operations.

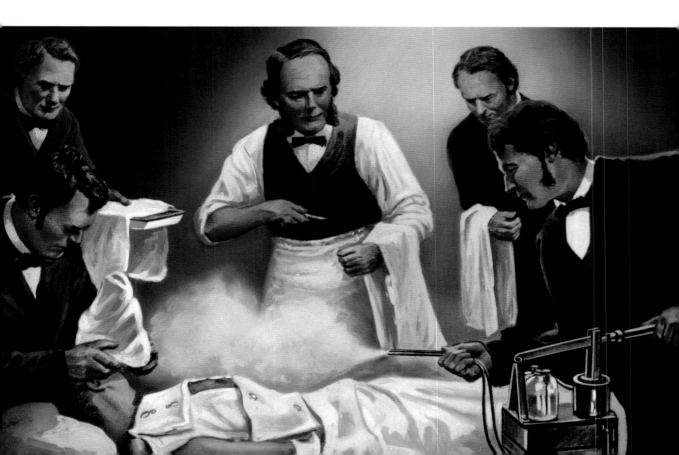

the French scientist Louis Pasteur discovered that microorganisms can cause disease. His discovery launched a new era in medical science.

Medical technologies have brought breakthroughs in the history of diagnosing (recognizing) and treating disease. The stethoscope was invented in France by René-Théophile-Hyacinthe Laënnec in 1816, allowing doctors to listen to sounds inside the body. The English physician Sir Thomas Allbutt invented the first medical thermometer, to measure the body's temperature, in 1866. These two inventions revolutionized medical care.

The development of anaesthetics in the nineteenth century gave surgeons a way to numb pain. By making patients unconscious during surgery, or by numbing a specific part of the body, surgeons could operate more slowly and carefully on patients than before. With anaesthesia, medical professionals developed refined surgical skills, carrying out increasingly complex and delicate procedures.

Technology and medicine advance together

Since the early twentieth century, medical science has advanced at an ever-accelerating pace, making use of nearly every new scientific and technical discovery. Recent studies of the atoms that make up matter, and of the small particles inside those atoms, have led to imaging technology that allows doctors to see inside the body. The most recent developments in robotics have led to improved surgical procedures. Breakthroughs in the understanding of genetic inheritance and the chemistry of life have allowed scientists to manipulate genes and even diseases themselves. Every advance takes people closer to achieving the age-old goal of humans – the desire to live long and healthy lives.

VIEWPOINT

Computers and medicine

Computerized systems have revolutionized many aspects of science. In medicine, the internet is affecting how care is delivered by hospitals, physicians and health centres:

'In the next ten years we can expect ... telesurgery [surgery using robotic tools controlled by a surgeon over the internet] in ... mainstream clinical practice ... [and] integrated electronic health records. The challenge for health professionals is to harness the new power at their disposal for the benefit of their patients.'

(H. Agius-Muscat, Director of Health Information, Government of Malta)

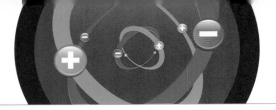

CHAPTER 2

High-Tech Hospitals

Two hundred years ago, an operating theatre was a horrifying place. Strong assistants held the patient down while the surgeon operated without anaesthetic in dirty conditions. If the patient survived the shock of the ordeal, he or she had a good chance of dying from infection. Modern surgery began with the arrival of anaesthetics and germ-killing antiseptics more than 150 years ago. In the 1840s, dentists and surgeons began to use fumes from ether to put patients to sleep during operations. The more powerful chloroform was first used in Edinburgh in 1847.

In the same year, the Hungarian doctor Ignaz Philipp Semmelweis observed that making doctors wash their hands between conducting autopsies (examinations of dead bodies) and delivering babies cut the death rate amongst new mothers. In 1867, the English surgeon Joseph Lister was the first to use carbolic acid, which kills bacteria, to sterilize instruments.

Telesurgery

In telesurgery, a robot performs an operation under the direction of a surgeon using remote control. The Da Vinci robot has arms that duplicate the movements of the human wrist. The surgeon's directions to the robot can be relayed over the internet. Because the surgeon doesn't have to be in the operating room, surgery can be performed by doctors who may be very far away from the patient. One of the first remote operations was carried out on a patient in Strasbourg, France, in 2001. The surgeon controlling the robot was in New York.

Machines in the operating theatre

Today, an operating theatre is a sterile (germ-free) environment packed with advanced technology to help the surgical team and the patient. During an operation, the patient's vital signs – their breathing, heart rate and blood pressure – are carefully monitored by computers connected to sensors on the patient. Computers also control the flow of anaesthetics and any other drugs to the patient.

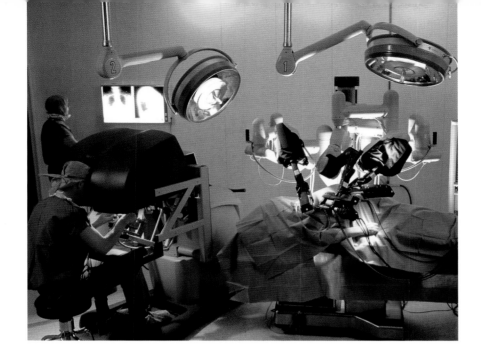

A surgeon carries out an operation using the Da Vinci surgical robot. The surgeon can see a three-dimensional image of the inside of the body on the screen.

A surgeon may use advanced medical robots to help perform delicate operations. Machinery such as the Da Vinci robot can wield tiny surgical tools with great precision. The surgeon directs the computerized tools, sometimes working through a tiny incision (cut) and using magnifying lenses. The system can also produce a three-dimensional image on a computer screen of the part of the body being operated on.

 PROS: USE OF MACHINES

Computer monitoring of patients gives accurate data and frees skilled staff to carry out other tasks. Telesurgery gives patients access to surgeons and specialists who may not be available locally. In the future, telesurgery may be used to perform operations on patients aboard planes, ships and even spacecraft.

 CONS: USE OF MACHINES

Some patients may be disturbed at the idea that their operation will be carried out by a robot, even though it is controlled by a human surgeon. Equally, some surgeons may feel that they are deskilled, or their skills are devalued, by using robotic tools.

New techniques in heart surgery

Improvements in surgical tools and techniques have enabled surgeons to carry out both more delicate processes and more daring, large-scale procedures. Surgeons can use new techniques such as laparoscopy, which involves making a small cut in the patient and passing a tube into the body. Some operations can be carried out using tools fed along the tube (see page 37).

Heart-lung machines in bypass surgery

During open-heart surgery (surgery that requires cutting into the heart), the patient's blood is routed through a heart-lung machine. The machine chills, pumps and aerates (gives oxygen to) the blood, performing the function of the heart and lungs, while the surgical team operates directly on the heart. This technique is used to perform heart bypass surgery. In some cases, patients have a quadruple bypass – in which all four main arteries to the heart are replaced with artificial tubes.

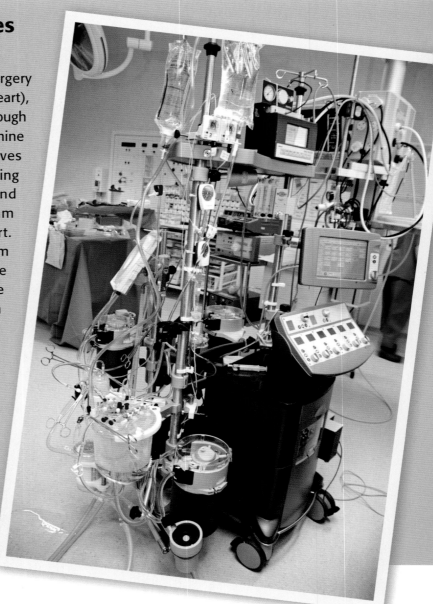

The heart-lung machine takes over the tasks of the heart and lungs during an operation. It aerates the blood, removes carbon dioxide from it and makes sure it is the right temperature.

Great advances in heart surgery have been made in recent years. Balloon angioplasty is used to treat coronary heart disease, when an artery (blood vessel) in the heart becomes blocked. In a laparoscopic operation, a long tube is connected to a tiny balloon that is fed through a blood vessel in the patient's thigh. The surgeon guides the tube to the clogged artery, then inflates the balloon to unblock it. Alternatively, a tiny drill can be used to remove the deposits in the artery.

Other techniques are much more invasive. In heart bypass surgery, the surgeon removes the blocked or damaged section of the artery and replaces it with an artificial tube. The heart has four valves that control the flow of blood through the body. Heart valve surgery involves fitting artificial valves inside the heart to replace those natural valves that have stopped working. These types of operation take many hours and are very complicated.

 PROS: HEART SURGERY

Some new surgical techniques are less invasive and therefore less stressful for patients than traditional procedures. Such surgery can often be performed more quickly and cheaply, and sometimes the patient needs to be in hospital only for the day of the procedure. Other techniques allow much more complex and demanding operations to take place. This can save lives – many patients whose conditions would have been inoperable 50 years ago can now be saved by major surgery using advanced techniques.

 CONS: HEART SURGERY

There is a risk that some patients may have a poor quality of life after their operations. They may have to take large quantities of drugs over many years, or they may need repeat surgery. Advanced procedures are very expensive and are not always successful. Some people think the huge sums involved would be better spent on an increased number of less invasive operations for people who could expect a better quality of life after surgery.

Florence Nightingale at work in the military hospital at Scutari during the Crimean War. Several aspects of modern hospital practice began with her work at this time.

Intensive care

Intensive-care units (ICUs) are special wards for patients who are critically ill. The idea of segregating the neediest patients was first introduced by the British nurse Florence Nightingale, when she was caring for wounded soldiers during the Crimean War (1853–6). The first modern intensive-care ward was established in Copenhagen, Denmark, by Bjørn Ibsen in 1953.

An ICU uses sophisticated equipment to monitor a patient's condition and keep him or her alive. Machines frequently carry out functions that the patient's body cannot manage, taking

Premature babies

VIEWPOINT

Sometimes considerable intervention is used to save preterm babies who need a lot of care. It does not always save their lives:

'A premature baby is as much a member of the human community as anybody else, and deserves the best care that's available. By and large this care has been extremely successful. There are thousands going into adulthood who previously wouldn't have done so. There are some children at the extremes, for whom intensive care can't provide hope, and who will not survive. In those circumstances it's best not to start.'

(John Wyatt, Professor of Neonatal Paediatrics, University College London Hospital, UK)

on the task of respiration (breathing), assisting the heart, pumping the blood or cleaning the blood by kidney dialysis. A steady, carefully regulated stream of drugs keeps the patient free of pain and tranquillized (calm and still). If a patient's condition takes a sudden turn for the worse, hospital staff can take emergency action – for example, to restart the patient's heart.

Special care baby units are ICUs to care for sick babies. Babies born before the full nine-month term of pregnancy (preterm or premature babies) may not be fully developed and often need some form of treatment. Machinery in the unit regulates temperature, delivers oxygen, feeds the baby through a tube and monitors the baby's vital signs (breathing, blood pressure and heart rate) around the clock.

 PROS: INTENSIVE-CARE UNITS

ICUs and special-care baby units have saved the lives of hundreds of thousands of people who would otherwise have died. Many more people have been saved from disabling conditions or impaired quality of life by the high level of care these units can offer.

 CONS: INTENSIVE-CARE UNITS

ICUs can keep people alive long beyond the point at which their bodies would naturally give up. Some patients have suffered such extreme damage they are never expected to recover normal brain function. A patient with severe brain damage may not be able to move, breathe or eat without technological assistance, and may not be able to think or communicate in any way. Relatives and doctors have to make difficult decisions about whether to suspend medical care and let these patients die. An extended legal battle in the United States surrounded the patient Terri Schiavo who suffered brain damage in 1990. Her husband wanted her life support discontinued, while her parents wanted her to be kept alive. She died in 2005 when life support was suspended.

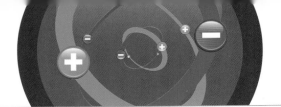

CHAPTER 3

Superhumans

People have long used simple aids to replace body parts lost to disease or accident. Wooden legs and hooks have been used for thousands of years, and spectacles were invented more than 700 years ago. During the twentieth century, the technology moved beyond these simplest aids to highly sophisticated technical replacements.

Inside the body

Advances in surgery have allowed replacement parts to be implanted into many areas of the body. One of the best-known implants is a heart pacemaker. This device replaces or supplements the heart's own mechanism for regulating the heartbeat. The first pacemaker to be implanted into a person's chest was developed in Sweden in 1958 by Rune Elmqvist and Åke Senning. Today, the newest pacemakers monitor and store information about the patient's condition. This information is sent wirelessly to a mobile phone communicator, which the patient carries. The communicator uses the mobile phone network to send updates to the patient's hospital, clinic or physician.

Today, many parts of the body can be replaced if they become injured or wear out. This coloured X-ray shows a replacement knee joint. The two metal ends to the bones show up in cream on the X-ray.

This means that the patient needs fewer check-ups. The pacemaker also alerts care workers if anything goes wrong.

Around 30 million Americans suffer from deteriorated and painful joints, such as hips and knees. Many have replacement joints to relieve pain and restore mobility.

Some of the newest types of implant aim to give some hearing or vision to patients who are deaf or blind. They use sensors to pick up sounds or light and convert them to electrical impulses which are sent to the person's brain.

Bionic eyes

A retinal implant is a tiny sliver of computer technology that is fitted into the retina – the light-sensitive surface at the back of the eye. The implant is worn with special glasses that have a digital camera and a laser. The camera captures an image which is sent into the eye as pulses of laser light. Two microchips in the implant convert the light pulses to electric signals. A set of electrodes in the implant sends the signals to the brain where they are interpreted in the same way as normal vision. So far, the first retinal implants have produced only low-resolution, blocky images.

 PROS: IMPLANTS AND REPLACEMENTS

Implants can restore people to an active life and enable them to be independent. Implants that give some vision or hearing will help to increase people's enjoyment of life. In the case of a pacemaker, the implant can greatly extend the patient's life expectancy.

 CONS: IMPLANTS AND REPLACEMENTS

Implants and replacement joints usually work well, but there can be problems. Between 1990 and 2002, out of 2.25 million patients fitted with pacemakers in the United States, 66 people died as a result of pacemaker failures. Some electrical equipment and items that contain magnets may interfere with pacemakers, so patients have to be careful to avoid such devices. If joints, pacemakers or implants malfunction or wear out, the patient has to undergo further invasive surgery to replace or repair them. Hearing implants involve invasive techniques and the results may only provide partial hearing, which can lead to frustration.

New limbs

Modern prosthetic (artificial) limbs look very like real limbs. Each prosthetic limb is matched to the individual's skin tone and body. Its 'skin' is very similar to real skin in both appearance and texture. Many new prosthetics are bionic, which means that they use electronic and mechanical devices to mimic how the body moves naturally.

The newest prosthetics in development use 'smart' technology to make them act more like real limbs. Computer chips take information from sensors to make the prosthetic respond just like a real limb. A robotic hand can adjust the power of its grip. A robotic leg can adapt its way of moving to suit rough terrain. Sensors in the fingertip or foot make that possible by communicating with a small computer chip implanted in the stump.

There is ongoing research into biohybrid limbs, which will incorporate remaining biological tissue – muscles, nerves and bone – into the bionic limb itself. Scientists are also developing limbs that make use of neurotechnology – technology that works with the body's nervous system. They are designing limbs which can be controlled by the signals that travel along the nerves. One method is to inject a tiny wireless microchip into remaining muscle that runs to the lost part of the limb. The microchip picks up signals from the nervous system and transmits them to the limb to make it move.

Future developments

VIEWPOINT

Researchers are beginning to bring together the fruits of research in different areas to produce truly 'smart' prosthetic limbs:

'We've got tissue engineering, neurotechnology, materials science, surgery. All of this work could come together in a biohybrid limb … My dream with this project is to allow someone who has lost an arm to brush their teeth or use a computer, or to allow someone who's lost a leg to climb stairs or ski again. I think we have the technology. We just need the courage to try it out.'

(Professor Ray Aaron, Professor of Orthopedics, Medical School of Brown University, USA)

Oscar Pistorius of South Africa competes in the 200 metres final on his prosthetic running blades at the 2008 Paralympic Games in Beijing, China. Pistorius won the gold medal.

 PROS: SOPHISTICATED PROSTHETICS

Sophisticated prosthetics can greatly increase people's mobility and independence. The latest prosthetics look very convincing and may help to stop people feeling self-conscious about their bodies. Some prosthetics are specially adapted to the individual's requirements, so an athlete may have running blades for competing but ordinary legs for everyday use, for example.

 CONS: SOPHISTICATED PROSTHETICS

Some patients find the connection between a sophisticated prosthetic limb and their body uncomfortable, and they may return to wearing a more traditional prosthetic. Tailored prosthetic limbs are very expensive to produce. This is a particular problem for children, because as a child grows it is vital to replace a prosthetic frequently. In countries where people have to pay for health care or health insurance, the latest prosthetic limbs are simply too expensive for many people to afford.

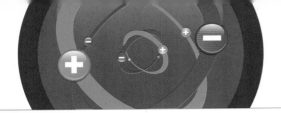

CHAPTER 4

Fighting Disease

Fighting illness and infection is the mainstay of medical care, and the impact of science and technology in this area has been immense. Our increased understanding about how disease is caused, how it affects the body and how it is transmitted between people has come from a long history of research.

In 1854, a British doctor called John Snow demonstrated that the cause of a terrible cholera epidemic in London was water from a particular pump. But although he showed that dirty water carried the disease, there was no firm understanding of how this happened. When Pasteur first suggested that microorganisms cause disease, he was ridiculed. The idea that tiny germs were making people ill was not accepted until the late 1860s. Viruses, which are many times smaller than bacteria, weren't even discovered until 1895. Since then, growing knowledge about bacteria and viruses has fed into the development of new drugs and treatments.

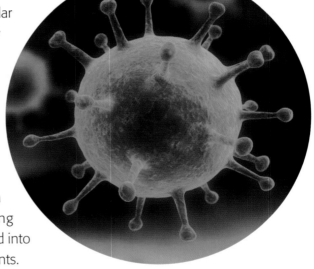

An artist's impression of a close-up view of a virus. Viruses grow and reproduce inside the cells of host organisms.

Bacteria and viruses

To experiment with diseases, medical researchers collect infected tissue and isolate disease-causing bacteria and viruses. Dangerous microorganisms are kept in a sterile, secure environment and are handled with great care. Bacteria are independent organisms, and colonies can be grown and studied. Viruses can survive only inside the cell of an organism, called a host. Research into viruses has increased since the invention of the powerful electron microscope in the 1930s.

Virus experiments

To understand viruses, scientists need to study them in the laboratory. This necessarily involves dealing with some very dangerous materials:

'Many influenza virologists [scientists who study viruses] remain nervous about creating and experimenting with a reconstructed 1918 Spanish flu virus, an extremely dangerous virus which disappeared from the world long ago. However, it cannot be denied that the information that has been derived from this experiment is exciting and represents an important milestone in understanding the severity of these highly pathogenic [disease-causing] types of influenza viruses.'

(Dr Jim Robertson, National Institute of Biological Standards and Control, UK)

➕ PROS: MEDICAL EXPERIMENTS

Experimentation with viruses and bacteria in the laboratory greatly extends our understanding of the diseases we have to combat. It has led to new treatments that both save lives and improve the quality of patients' lives.

A scientist working with a sample of the flu virus that caused a pandemic in 1918. It affected a fifth of the world's population and killed around 50 million people.

➖ CONS: MEDICAL EXPERIMENTS

Keeping deadly microbes in laboratories can be dangerous, and some researchers have fallen ill or died as a result of laboratory accidents. The viruses that cause smallpox and Spanish flu no longer exist in nature, but vials of these deadly viruses are kept in laboratories and used for research. Some people worry that such viruses might be released by accident, or may be stolen and turned into a terrorist weapon.

Medical research

Once a treatment has been developed in the laboratory, the next stage often involves testing on animals. If this is successful, the final stage consists of clinical trials, in which the treatment is tried out first on healthy people and then on real patients.

Experimenting on animals is not considered acceptable by some people. They object on ethical grounds, or say that the response of an animal's body is not a good guide to how a human body may react. Clinical trials on people may also go wrong. In 2006, six men who were taking part in a drug trial organized by a German company became seriously ill. The worst affected spent 16 days in a coma and lost toes and fingers as a result.

Coping with cancer

There are many different types of cancer, but they are all characterized by the uncontrolled growth of cells in a part of the body. Such rapid growth usually results in one or more tumours. About 12 million new

This photograph, taken through an electron microscope, shows a breast cancer cell in the process of dividing in two.

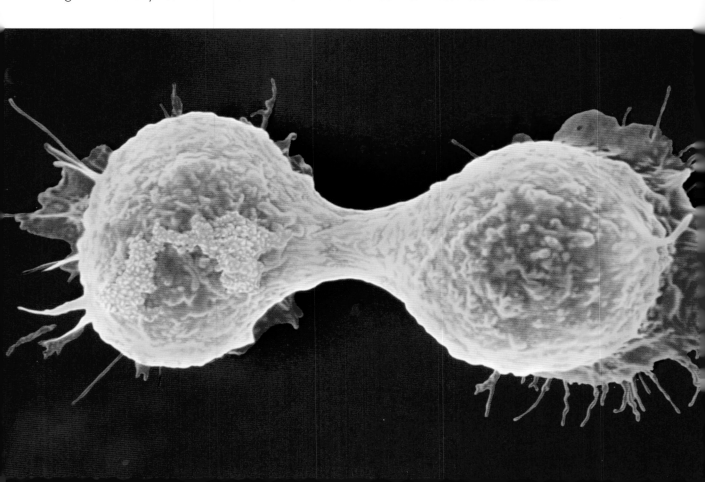

cases of cancer are diagnosed worldwide each year, and half a million people in the United States die of cancer every year.

Modern treatments for cancer can often cure a patient, or at least extend a patient's life, if the disease is caught early enough. There are several ways to treat cancer. Radiotherapy uses radiation to kill cancerous cells. Chemotherapy uses strong chemicals to 'poison' cancerous cells. Both methods have unpleasant side effects because they also affect non-cancerous cells. Newer treatments try to target the cancer cells without harming other cells. They involve delivering tiny amounts of drugs or radioactive materials directly to the site of the cancer.

A Trojan horse against cancer

An experimental treatment for cancer involves using nanoparticles – particles smaller than a millionth the size of a pinhead – to carry anti-cancer drugs directly into cancer cells. The nanoparticles fool the cancer cell by appearing to deliver useful nutrients. Once inside the cell, they release strong chemotherapy drugs to kill the tumour.

 PROS: CANCER TREATMENTS

Cancer treatments extend lives and save many people from a very unpleasant and painful death. In some areas, extensive research and development has led to a huge increase in survival rates. Since 1960, for instance, advanced medical care has led to survival rates for childhood leukaemia (cancer of the white blood cells) rising from less than 10 percent to around 75 percent or more.

 CONS: CANCER TREATMENTS

In some cases, the treatment for a particular type of cancer causes as much distress as the disease itself, and offers only a few months of extended life. For this reason, some patients prefer to let the cancer take its natural course. The high cost of new treatments means that they are often not available to everyone. News of breakthroughs in cancer research raises the hopes of all patients, but some treatments will not work and others will not be available for many years.

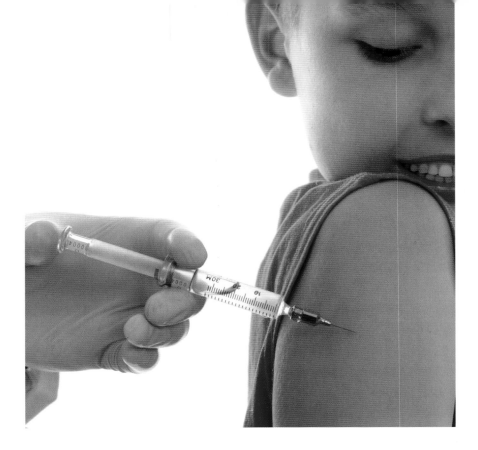

A physician prepares to inject a vaccine into a young patient.

Avoiding disease

People can protect themselves against some diseases with vaccinations or by using prophylactics (drugs or treatments that prevent disease).

Vaccination involves giving a person a very small amount of a disease-causing virus or bacteria that has been weakened or killed. The vaccine won't give the person the disease, but it will prompt the body to develop antibodies that will fight the disease. Antibodies are made by the immune system to fight infections and diseases. Once they develop, antibodies remain in the immune system to fight that particular disease should the body encounter it again.

The principle of vaccination was first used in Asia to provide protection against smallpox. But it was a British doctor, Edward Jenner, who in 1796 introduced a safe smallpox vaccine when he discovered that people exposed to the less dangerous disease of cowpox developed immunity to smallpox. There are now vaccines against many diseases. Children around the world are routinely vaccinated against previously common and deadly diseases such as diphtheria and measles.

Besides vaccines, some medicines can be taken as prophylactics to prevent the development of disease. Aspirin is often taken by people at risk of heart disease, for example, because it helps to prevent blood clotting. Prophylactic drugs work by changing conditions in the body to make it inhospitable to a viral or bacterial infection, or to prevent something going wrong.

 PROS: VACCINATION

Some diseases have been almost wiped out by vaccination, and smallpox has been eradicated completely. Travellers can be vaccinated against diseases common in areas they are visiting, and health workers can be protected against hepatitis, which they could contract from the body fluids of patients.

 CONS: VACCINATION

Like all medicines, some vaccines can have side effects. Often these are minor, but occasionally people can become quite ill. If people are worried about a vaccine, they may refuse it (see page 47). Some diseases, particularly those caused by viruses, change so quickly that a vaccine is effective for only a short time. The influenza vaccine, for example, has to be developed afresh each year.

Genetically-engineered bananas may be used to deliver a chlolera vaccine.

Health in a banana

Vaccines need to be kept cool and sterile, so taking them to remote and inaccessible regions of hot countries is often very difficult. In response, researchers are developing new ways of delivering vaccines. They have used genetic engineering techniques (changing the genes in an organism) to create bananas that contain a cholera vaccine, spinach that contains a rabies vaccine, and a hepatitis B vaccine that can be carried in bananas, carrots or potatoes. In each case, eating the food delivers the vaccine and gives people protection from the disease.

Sir Alexander Fleming, who discovered penicillin, at work in his laboratory at St Mary's Hospital in London, UK.

New medicines

Since Pasteur demonstrated the role of bacteria in illness, there has been great progress in fighting bacterial diseases. Pasteur discovered that bacteria could be killed by heating (pasteurization). From 1867, the British surgeon Joseph Lister used carbolic acid to sterilize instruments and operating theatres. Sterilization greatly reduces infection after surgery.

Antibiotics are substances that kill or prevent the growth of bacteria. Some work against only a few bacteria but others, called broad-spectrum antibiotics, are effective against many. The first broad-spectrum antibiotic, penicillin, was discovered accidentally by Alexander Fleming in 1928. Since then, many antibiotics have been developed and are used for the treatment of both people and animals.

Antibiotics are effective only against bacteria, so they cannot be used to treat diseases that are caused by viruses. Viruses enter a cell and have the potential to reproduce themselves, then burst out and infect other cells. Antiviral drugs prevent a virus from breaking into a cell, or prevent the copies from breaking out. Today, detailed knowledge of the chemistry and life cycles of bacteria and viruses allows researchers to develop new treatments.

PROS: ANTIBIOTICS

Antibiotics have given us cures for many conditions. The use of antibiotics has reduced infection after surgery or injury and saved millions of lives around the world. The use of antibiotics in farming has also helped to increase the yields of meat and dairy products by keeping farm animals healthy and productive.

 CONS: ANTIBIOTICS

The overuse of antibiotics in both humans and animals has led to the development of antibiotic-resistant strains of some diseases. Small amounts of antibiotic residue are present in many people's bodies, left over from treatments, and taken in through eating food from treated animals. These small quantities have, over time, led to bacteria building up resistance to the drugs. Infections caused by antibiotic-resistant bacteria include methicillin-resistant *Staphylococcus aureus* (MRSA) and *Clostridium difficile* (see page 50), as well as new forms of tuberculosis. They are all extremely difficult to control and treat.

The dangers of overuse

VIEWPOINT

An expert warns about the dangers of the overuse of drugs such as antibiotics and antivirals:

'We know from past experience that when we start using any antimicrobial drug excessively, that resistance to that drug eventually appears. Given the fact that there are very few new antimicrobial drugs being discovered, the message is that we really need to learn how to use the available drugs better … It's easy to get into a mindset of just using them for any trivial condition. We are undoubtedly overusing these drugs.'

(Professor Ronald Polk, Chairman of the Department of Pharmacy, Virginia Commonwealth University, USA)

Planning for pandemics

A pandemic is an outbreak of disease that spreads over a huge area such as a continent, sometimes the whole world. From 1348 to 1350, around a third of the population of Europe died of bubonic and other forms of plague, known as the Black Death. Between 1918 and 1920, around 50 million people died in a worldwide pandemic of Spanish flu. Flu pandemics recur at irregular intervals, and there will undoubtedly be another at some point.

To help prepare for and combat a possible pandemic, researchers examine body tissue from patients who suffered or died from pandemic illnesses. In the case of flu, they use detailed knowledge of the chemistry of the virus to work out how it attacks cells and how it could be controlled. Computers are used to predict how the disease might spread, how many people would be affected, what the social and economic impacts would be and how health services would cope with the workload. Drug manufacturers try to prepare vaccines or cures in advance. They also plan how they would produce the massive quantities of drugs necessary to fight a pandemic. People at high risk, along with health-care workers, would need to be vaccinated at the first signs of an outbreak.

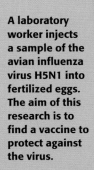

A laboratory worker injects a sample of the avian influenza virus H5N1 into fertilized eggs. The aim of this research is to find a vaccine to protect against the virus.

PROS: PANDEMIC PLANNING

Modelling and planning help governments and health services prepare for pandemics, and encourage the development of new drugs. Government and international agencies work together to tackle what may be a global problem.

 CONS: PANDEMIC PLANNING

Publicity about possible pandemics can cause panic. In 2003, when cases of a deadly strain of avian flu started to appear in Asia, people around the world panicked. Governments, corporations and even wealthy individuals began to stockpile flu antiviral drugs. This drained the world's supply, leading to shortages in areas where the drugs were already needed. A panic that turns out to be unfounded can also make people less likely to respond next time there is an alert.

Avian influenza

VIEWPOINT

In Asia there have been some cases of a strain of influenza which affects birds, called H5N1, passing from poultry to humans. The result in humans is serious illness and frequently death. At the moment, the disease does not easily spread from person to person, but scientists worry that this situation may change:

'The emergence of the H5N1 avian influenza virus … has raised concerns that it or another virus might mutate into a virulent [extremely harmful] strain that could lead to an influenza pandemic. Experts predict that a severe pandemic could overwhelm the nation's health-care system, requiring the rationing of limited resources.'
(US Government Accountability Office, September 2008)

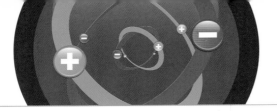

CHAPTER 5

Genetics

Farmers have used artificial selection for thousands of years to breed more productive crops and farm animals, but with little understanding of how it actually worked. The first insight came with the work of Gregor Mendel, an Austrian monk who demonstrated the principles of inherited characteristics in 1865, after experimenting with pea plants. The suggestion that inherited characteristics were carried by chromosomes appeared in 1902. The structure of the chemical deoxyribonucleic acid (DNA), which makes up chromosomes and carries genetic information, was discovered by Francis Crick, James Watson and Rosalind Franklin in 1953. The Human Genome Project, which aims to map the function of all human genetic material, began in 1990. Knowledge of genetics – characteristics that pass from generation to generation – has significant implications for medicine. It can help us predict or avoid disease, develop cures and begin to understand how we might be able to help the body to fix itself.

Stem cells

When a human egg is fertilized, it begins to divide, making more and more cells. At first, these are stem cells – they have the potential to grow into any kind of cell needed to make a human. Later, they begin to differentiate, making different types of cells to form a heart, a liver or skin, for example. The ability of stem cells to develop into other types of cell gives them huge potential in medicine. One

Growing stem cells

A supply of stem cells is needed for research and therapy. Instead of harvesting lots of stem cells, scientists grow a 'line' (a cell that produces more cells, which themselves produce more cells) of stem cells in the laboratory. Once a line is established, it can provide an unending supply of stem cells for research or therapy. The first line of human stem cells was grown in 2006. In 2008, scientists grew stem cells for various incurable inherited diseases, which will help them find treatments for these diseases.

day, an injection of stem cells could be used to regrow damaged nerves or heart tissue, for instance. For now, stem cells are valuable in research. Many serious medical conditions are caused by problems with cell division and differentiation. Studying stem cells helps medical researchers find out how these processes work and how they can go wrong.

Stem cells can be taken from embryos, or collected from blood in the umbilical cord after a baby is born (cord blood). Partially differentiated stem cells can be taken from adults.

A photograph taken with an electron microscope of two human embryonic stem cells.

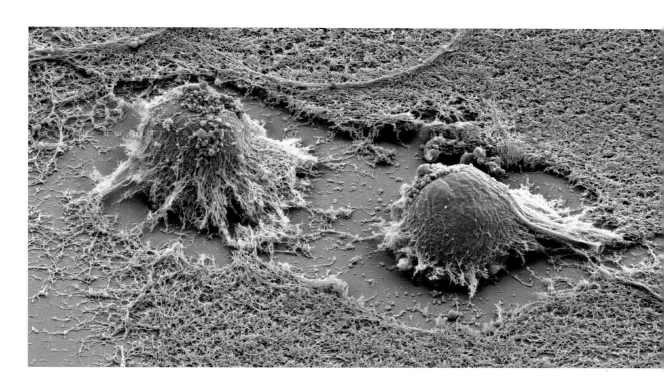

PROS: STEM CELLS

Scientists hope stem cells will offer a safe way of helping the body mend itself. If the body grows new tissue, there is no known risk of rejection or infection. At the moment, some blood diseases can be treated with stem cells obtained from cord blood. In the future, disorders such as Parkinson's disease and Alzheimer's might also be treated with stem cells.

CONS: STEM CELLS

Stem cells are most easily harvested from fertilized eggs. Such eggs have the potential, if implanted in a woman, to become babies. The use of stem cells that come from embryos raises complex practical and ethical problems. Research on adult and cord blood supplies of stem cells is less controversial. However, there are questions about how cord blood should be used, too. While some cord blood is stored in public banks, there are also private banks where parents can pay to keep cord blood from their child, or children. Public banks are a vital resource if this technology is to benefit the general population.

Genetic screening

Until recently, anyone with a history of hereditary disease in their family had no sure way of knowing whether they would become ill – they just had to wait and see. Huntington's chorea is an example of such a disease. It causes disability and early death, but symptoms do not emerge until a person is in their thirties or forties. Someone with a parent who has Huntington's chorea has a 50 percent chance of developing the disease. The genes that produce some inherited diseases, including Huntington's chorea, are now known. People who are at risk can be screened to see if they have the genes that will lead to them developing the disease.

Sometimes, people carry and pass on a genetic disease without suffering from it themselves. Cystic fibrosis is an example of this type of disease. When carriers plan to have children, they may choose to use in vitro fertilization (IVF). In this procedure, the eggs are fertilized outside the body, and the resulting embryos can be screened before implantation in the womb. Only embryos that do not carry the disease are implanted in the mother to grow.

Saved by a sister

'Saviour siblings' are babies that have been chosen, using IVF and genetic screening, specifically to provide tissue for transplant into a sibling (brother or sister) who is suffering from a genetic disorder. The new baby is healthy, and its tissue is a good match for the sibling. Often, a transfusion of cord blood is all that is needed from the new baby.

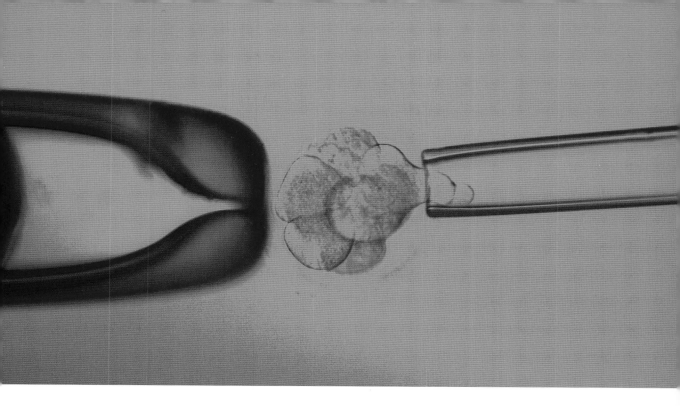

This eight-celled embryo has been produced by IVF. One cell is being removed (right) in order to screen the embryo for genetic disorders.

 PROS: GENETIC SCREENING

Genetic screening may spare people the agony of waiting to see if they will develop the symptoms of a disease. If people know they are at risk of developing an illness, they may be able to take precautionary measures, such as adjusting their lifestyle, taking drugs or having surgery. Screening and IVF programmes can ensure that people with a high risk of passing on a genetic disorder can make an informed decision about whether to start or continue with a pregnancy.

 CONS: GENETIC SCREENING

For some people, the certainty that they will develop an incurable disease is more stressful than the worry of not knowing. The knowledge that a person (or unborn baby) is free from one genetic defect does not mean he or she will be free from others. There is also a risk that genetic information will lead to discrimination. People may find it difficult to get work, or insurance, if it is known that they will or may develop a serious condition.

Scientists at work in a plant that produces human insulin from microorganisms. The microorganisms are grown in the large vats (containers) shown here.

Genetic engineering

Genetic engineering involves changing the genetic make-up of an organism, or changing the effect its genes have on the organism. There are several applications for genetic engineering in medicine and health. One important advance has been the ability to change bacteria and other microorganisms for use in medicine. For example, people with diabetes are unable to produce

Changing genes

To make a genetically modified organism scientists take DNA from one organism and splice, or join, it into the DNA of another. This is called recombinant DNA. The production of insulin from bacteria, introduced in 1977, was the first commercial use of this technology. The human gene for producing insulin is spliced into the DNA of a bacterium. The bacterium is grown in a vat of nutrients. As it reproduces, it makes exact copies of itself, creating both bacteria and insulin.

insulin, a hormone that controls the level of sugar in their blood. For many years, the insulin used in injections to help people with diabetes came from animals. Today, it is possible to obtain insulin in large quantities from a type of bacterium that has been genetically engineered.

Gene therapy, treating medical conditions by altering genes, is a promising area of medical research. This technique would allow medical professionals to 'correct' an inherited defect or change a genetic condition before birth. Turning off or disabling a gene so that it can't take effect in a person could prevent the development of an inherited disease, or stop a cancer growing.

 PROS: CHANGING GENES

Using genetic engineering to make drugs such as insulin in large volumes makes the treatment of some conditions cheaper and easier to provide. Other medical uses for genetic engineering include modifying foods to deliver vaccines or additional nutrients (see pages 21 and 52). It may be possible to reduce or eradicate populations of some disease-carrying insects by introducing genetically-engineered strains of insect that cannot transmit diseases to humans.

 CONS: CHANGING GENES

Some people are concerned that it may be ethically wrong, or dangerous, to make changes to the genes of people or other organisms. Screening to make sure a child is disease-free at birth seems reasonable, but the technology also allows people to determine characteristics based on preference rather than health. We do not fully understand how genes interact with each other, so there could be unforeseen consequences to genetic engineering. The high cost of genetic engineering means that the companies developing techniques and products want to retain ownership of them, so that they can profit from the investments they have made. This means that the benefits may be available only to wealthy people in economically developed countries.

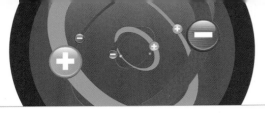

CHAPTER 6

Looking inside the Body

When the German physicist Wilhelm Roentgen made an X-ray of the bones in his wife's hand in 1895, he began an era of imaging in medicine. Today, X-rays are only one of the many ways of seeing inside a patient's body.

Imaging technologies

X-rays are routinely used to provide images of bones that are broken or diseased. Chest X-rays help to diagnose pneumonia and lung cancer. CAT (computerized axial tomography) scans and MRI (magnetic resonance imaging) are used to take pictures of soft tissue. CAT scanners use X-rays together with a chemical contrast agent which penetrates different tissues to different degrees. A machine rotates around the body, collecting images from X-rays that pass through the body. A computer then builds a three-dimensional picture from these images. The first CAT scan of a patient's brain took place in 1972.

An MRI scanner uses a strong magnetic field to create images of the body. MRI scans are widely used to diagnose damage to the brain, muscles and cardiovascular system (heart and blood), and to look at cancers. The first MRI scan was produced in 1977.

MRI scanner

The MRI scanner is used to get a picture of soft tissue, such as muscles and organs. It uses a very strong magnetic field – up to 60,000 times as strong as the Earth's magnetic field – to align the direction of hydrogen nuclei within the body. Radio waves are then used to change the alignment of the nuclei, and these changes are measured by a scanner. A computer can build up an image of soft tissue from the measurements.

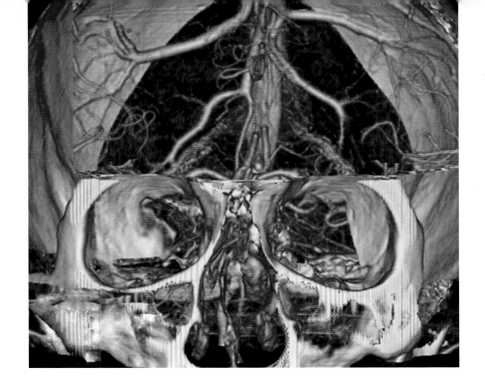

An MRI scan showing
the blood vessels in
the brain. Images such
as this are often used
to find aneurysms
(bulging blood vessels)
in the brain.

 PROS: IMAGING

Imaging techniques help diagnose illnesses and identify damaged
tissue. Identifying such problems at an early stage can be crucial for
successful treatment. Improved information about the brain gained
from imaging has led to greater understanding of how the brain works,
and of mental illness and brain damage.

 CONS: IMAGING

Some CAT and MRI patients have a serious allergic reaction to the
contrast agent used. The agent can also cause kidney damage, and is
not suitable for all patients. People with a pacemaker or other metal
implant cannot have MRI scans because of the use of magnetic fields,
although newer designs of implant are being made MRI-safe. An MRI
scan can be uncomfortable: it is noisy, and the patient has to lie still
for up to an hour in an enclosed space. Many people experience
twitching caused by the switching of the magnetic field. The images
sometimes reveal lumps that turn out to be harmless, but their
discovery can cause stress for patients until the issue is resolved.

Looking at working systems

A PET (positron emission tomography) scan measures body functions, such as blood flow and oxygen use, as they happen. This allows doctors to see how the body is working and detect any problems. The patient ingests or is injected with a substance used by the body (often a sugar) which contains a low-risk radioactive chemical. This chemical emits energy at a steady rate. The energy it gives off in different places is measured by a scanner and then translated into an image by a computer. The result is a detailed image of the inner workings of the body. A PET scan is often used to diagnose cancer

PET scans for Alzheimer's

Alzheimer's is a disease that causes slow mental degeneration. A new technique for diagnosing Alzheimers uses a radioactive or 'glowing' dye and a PET scanner. The dye binds to a protein produced in areas of the brain affected by Alzheimer's. These areas show up in red on the scan. It is the first clinical test for Alzheimer's. Previously, all diagnosis was based purely on assessing the patient's symptoms.

An ultrasound image of an unborn baby developing inside the mother's womb.

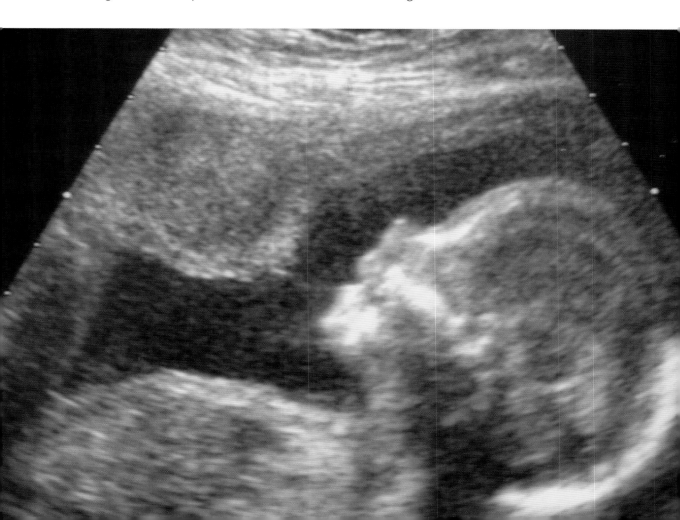

and brain disease. It is also used in research to investigate how healthy bodies function.

Ultrasound and thermal imaging also allow a medical team to see working and moving structures inside the body. Ultrasound sends sound waves into the body and creates an image from the echo. It shows the density of soft and hard tissue in organs, muscles, tendons and the eyes. It is commonly used in pregnancy to check the position and development of the foetus. Ultrasound is also used by surgeons to help them guide fine needles through the body. This technique is often used to do biopsies, the removal of cells or tissue for examination.

Thermal imaging (thermography) creates an image from heat emitted by the body. Cell activity and generated heat are greater near cancerous tumours. Thermography is often used to identify breast cancers. Thermal imaging is also a useful research tool because it shows how the body works during different types of activity.

 PROS: ULTRASOUND AND THERMAL IMAGING

These imaging procedures can lead to early diagnosis of conditions such as blockages and tumours. Ultrasound is useful for the dating of pregnancy and to diagnose any problems that may require immediate treatment or may have implications for the birth. It can reveal multiple births (twins and triplets, for instance) and ectopic pregnancies (when the foetus begins to develop outside the womb, and cannot survive). The images produced by these technologies have provided invaluable information about structures deep in the body, extending our understanding of how the body works.

 CONS: ULTRASOUND AND THERMAL IMAGING

These safe technologies have few negative impacts. However, all of them can occasionally reveal symptoms that require further investigation that are often found to be harmless. Additional testing increases the cost of treatment and is often a source of needless worry for patients.

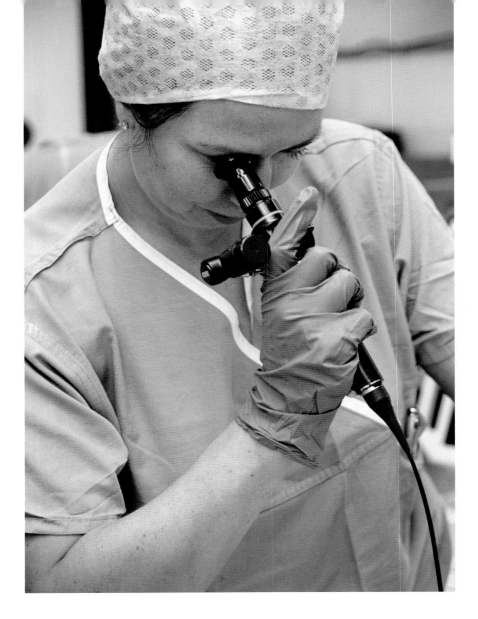

A surgeon uses an endoscope to see inside a patient's body. The endoscope has a camera and a light source, so the surgeon can take photographs.

Cameras in the body

From the early 1950s, a British physicist called Harold Hopkins worked on the technique of using fibre-optic cables to see deep inside the body. Hopkins finalized his design in 1967. The modern endoscope is a long tube that contains fibre-optic cables which take light into the body, and allow doctors to view, video or photograph internal

Super skinny endoscope

The newest endoscopes, developed by an Australian researcher called Martijn van Eijkelenborg in 2004, are thin enough to fit along blood vessels. They are only half a millimetre wide and are made from a single fibre with hundreds of holes running along its length. An ordinary endoscope is a bundle of fibres about five millimetres across.

organs. It is commonly used to investigate intestinal and gynaecological complaints. To look inside the gut, the patient is partially sedated before the endoscope is passed down the throat.

A laparoscope is a type of endoscope with a shorter tube which is inserted through a small incision, often in the abdomen. In laparoscopic surgery, also called keyhole surgery, a surgeon uses small instruments to work inside the body through a very small incision. Both endoscopy and laparoscopy can be used to take biopsies, to retrieve foreign objects that have been swallowed or inhaled, or to aid surgeons in placing implants.

 PROS: ENDOSCOPY AND LAPAROSCOPY

Endoscopy has largely replaced the use of barium meals to investigate blockages or lumps in the intestines. Previously, the patient was fed an unpleasant solution of barium sulphate, which shows up on X-rays, and the abdomen was then X-rayed to reveal any problems. Both endoscopy and laparoscopy are minimally invasive and do not require the use of X-rays. They provide a considerable aid to diagnosis and can often be used instead of investigative surgery. Laparoscopic surgery is also less invasive than open surgery. Patients suffer less pain and damage to muscles and skin, and often only need a short stay in hospital.

 CONS: ENDOSCOPY AND LAPAROSCOPY

Occasionally organs are damaged accidentally by an endoscope or laparoscope. Patients are sedated for endoscopy, but may suffer a sore throat and other ill effects after the procedure. Laparoscopic surgery usually requires several incisions, so there is pain at more than one site and more than one wound to heal. Patients are often only admitted to hospital for a day for laparoscopic surgery, and complications can sometimes occur after they have been sent home. Laparoscopic surgery also uses costly equipment and requires special training, so it is not available everywhere.

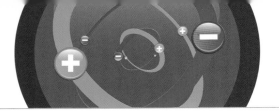

CHAPTER 7

Organ Transplants

Some damage to body parts cannot be repaired, but a damaged organ can sometimes be replaced. A surgeon may suggest that a patient has a transplant to replace a faulty organ. Organs for transplant come from people who have chosen to donate their organs after death, often from people who have died in accidents.

Heart and lung transplants

Experiments to transplant organs and tissues began long ago. The first successful transplant was performed in 1668 by a Dutchman, Job van Meeneren, when he took bone from a dog to repair a human cranium. In 1967, a South African surgeon called Christiaan Barnard carried out the first successful heart transplant. The patient survived for 18 days before dying of pneumonia. The first heart-lung transplant took place in Britain in 1983; the patient survived for 13 days. Today, microsurgery techniques, heart-lung bypass machines and

VIEWPOINT

Scientific breakthrough?

In 1967, Christiaan Barnard made this comment about the first heart transplant:

'[The heart is] a very easy organ to transplant. There will be much greater scientific breakthroughs in medicine, because the heart transplant was not a scientific breakthrough. It was a technical breakthrough.'

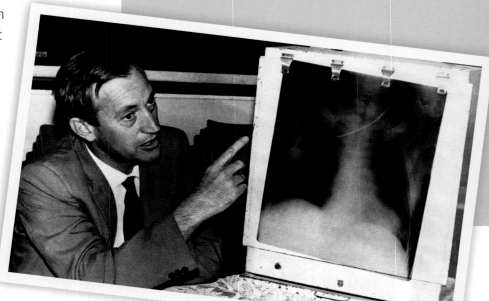

Surgeon Christiaan Barnard shows an X-ray of the chest of the first heart-transplant patient Louis Washansky.

sophisticated anti-rejection drugs allow surgeons to replace the heart and lungs of a patient with a much better chance of success.

The list of people waiting for a donor organ is long but the number of donors is fairly small. At present, there is such high demand for transplant organs that around 60 percent of patients die while waiting for an organ. Using organs from other animals (most likely pigs) could end the shortage. The largest obstacle to xenotransplant (the transplant of an organ between species) is rejection of the new organ, but genetic engineering may be able to overcome this problem.

 PROS: TRANSPLANTS

Transplants restore many patients to full health, and many people can live active and independent lives after surgery. There have been spin-off benefits for medical science in the development of microsurgery techniques and greater understanding of how the immune system works.

 CONS: TRANSPLANTS

The shortage of organs for donation has led to unethical practices in some countries, including the sale of organs on international markets and the harvesting of organs without the consent of donors' families.

Patients need to take powerful anti-rejection drugs until the body has accepted the organ. If the organ is rejected, the patient must take anti-rejection drugs for life. These suppress the immune system, making people vulnerable to other infections. Sometimes, the drugs cannot stop rejection and the organ must be removed. The risk of rejection varies with different organs – there is a low risk with cornea transplants, for instance, but a higher risk with kidney transplants.

Faced with the possibility of xenotransplants, some people worry about feeling 'less human', or about new kinds of infections or complications. Some people also have religious or personal beliefs which make transplants from animals unacceptable to them.

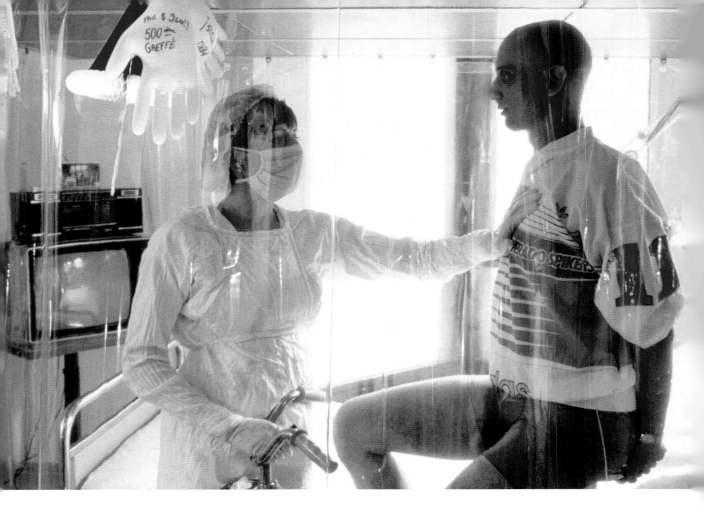

Transplants from living donors

Not all transplant donors are dead. For transplants that do not require a complete organ, a living donor is often used. Living donors can give skin, for example. They can also give a kidney, as people need only one of their two kidneys to live normally, or part of their liver. The donor's own liver will regrow and more healthy liver will grow in the patient. Often, kidney or liver transplants are from donors related to the patient. Blood relatives are more likely to have compatible organs, reducing the risk of rejection.

Some conditions that require a liver transplant are caused by the patient's own behaviour – such as damage from a paracetamol overdose, or cirrhosis caused by excessive drinking. There is some debate about whether people who may be considered responsible for their condition should be equally eligible for donor organs as patients who are ill through no fault of their own.

Bone marrow and blood are transfused rather than transplanted. Bone marrow and blood are drawn from living donors, carefully matched to a

A patient who has received a bone marrow transplant uses an exercise bicycle inside his sterile room while recovering from treatment.

recipient, and then pumped directly into the bloodstream of the recipient. Bone marrow is used to treat leukaemia and other blood diseases. The marrow contains stem cells which can produce more blood cells. The recipient produces healthy blood cells, replacing their own diseased cells.

As with other transplants (except blood), tissue from living donors can be rejected by the body so the patient needs to take anti-rejection drugs. In the past, undiagnosed infections have sometimes been spread by blood or bone marrow transfusions. HIV/AIDs and hepatitis have both been passed on through blood products. Today, all donated tissue is screened for known risks – but the small chance of an as-yet unknown risk emerging is always present.

 PROS: LIVING DONORS

A living donor means patients don't have to wait for someone to die before they can receive an organ. Many people who are able to donate liver, kidney or bone marrow to save a relative or a stranger feel privileged and pleased to be able to help.

 CONS: LIVING DONORS

In most countries it is illegal to buy and sell human organs. However, the demand for organs is so great that there is an illegal market for human organs. Desperately poor people, often living in developing nations such as India, may decide to sell their organs. This puts their own health at risk and raises ethical questions about whether body parts should be bought and sold.

Split liver transplant

As well as splitting a liver between a donor and a recipient, the liver of a dead donor can be split between two patients. The liver may be split equally between two adults, or split so that one-third is given to a small child and two-thirds to an adult.

Hands and faces

Recent advances in transplant technologies, particularly in microsurgery, have made many new types of transplant possible. In 1998 the first hand transplant was carried out in France. In July 2008, a man in Germany received two new arms in the first transplant operation of its kind. The first face transplant took place in France in 2005. A woman who had been mauled by a dog had a transplant to rebuild her face. Transplants of exterior body parts such as hands and faces involve extremely intricate surgery. Not all transplants are to remedy illness and damage. People suffering hair loss may choose to have hair follicles (the pores from which hairs grow) transplanted from the back of the head to bald patches. Skin grafts are frequently carried out to conceal scars or help to heal large wounds.

 PROS: NEW TRANSPLANTS

People who receive transplants of body parts such as hands and feet have their mobility and independence restored. Those who have a retinal transplant are able to see again. People who need face transplants are very badly disfigured, usually by accidents, and have often had to endure stares and even unkindness. A transplant can completely transform the life of the patient.

 CONS: NEW TRANSPLANTS

As with all transplants, patients have to take anti-rejection drugs and follow a strict regime to keep their new body part healthy. External body parts are on display all the time. Patients are constantly reminded that they have someone else's hand or face and some can find this very disturbing. If the transplanted part does not match the recipient's skin well, this problem is even more pronounced. The first hand transplant patient had the hand amputated in 2001, three years after the transplant operation. He could not cope with his body's rejection of the hand, the embarrassment it caused him, and his feeling of being 'emotionally detached' from it.

Frenchwoman Isabelle Dinoire received the world's first face transplant in 2005, after being horrifically disfigured in an attack by a dog.

Face transplant

A face transplant involves removing the skin, fat and blood vessels from the face of the patient and replacing them with those of the donor. All the blood vessels and nerves in the new face are connected to the patient's own face. The operation takes around 14 hours to complete. However, the structure of a face is determined by its bones, cartillage and muscles, so the patient's new face does not look the same as it did on the original donor.

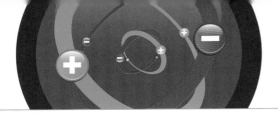

CHAPTER 8

Public and Private Health

Health is not just a private issue. Governments and health authorities deal with the health of whole populations. They oversee health-care services and fund health initiatives. They educate people about health and promote campaigns to prevent illness. Today, some countries provide free health care for the whole population, funded by taxes. In other countries, people must pay for their own medical care or take out insurance to cover their health costs.

Computers and health care

In many countries, health records are stored centrally on computers. When people are ill or have accidents, their health records are immediately available to any hospital or doctor who treats them. Computers can also help doctors diagnose illness and choose treatments. Large databases hold information about a huge number of conditions, their symptoms, treatment and prognosis (prospects for recovery). A database can store far more information than any single individual can recall. Medical workers also use computers and the internet to share knowledge with other professionals, and to ask for advice from experts in particular fields.

For individuals, the internet provides a wealth of information about medical conditions. There are also online support groups where sufferers and their families can share information about dealing with an illness, and its impact on their lives.

A doctor uses a computer terminal at the bedside to update the records of a patient's care.

PROS: COMPUTERS AND HEALTH

Instant access to computerized patient records can save lives. It can tell health workers if someone is already taking medication, has a known condition or is allergic to any particular medicine. Online support groups are particularly valuable for people with rare conditions who may otherwise never encounter fellow sufferers. Some patients find details of new treatments which their own caregiver may not know about. Health services and hospitals put information online to help patients, reducing the need for people to visit health-care providers to resolve simple issues.

 CONS: COMPUTERS AND HEALTH

Some people try to diagnose their conditions themselves using information from the internet. If they get it wrong, they may worry unnecessarily or – worse – neglect a dangerous condition. Self-prescribing and buying drugs online can be dangerous. Some information online is inaccurate or dangerous. Some sites about eating disorders actually promote the disorder and encourage unhealthy behaviour. Many people worry that computerized medical records are at risk of loss or theft and that very sensitive information may not be kept securely.

Computerized health care

VIEWPOINT

In January 2009, US president Barack Obama spoke of his plans to introduce computerized health-care records across the United States:

'This will cut waste, eliminate red tape, and reduce the need to repeat expensive medical tests … It won't just save billions of dollars and thousands of jobs – it will save lives by reducing the deadly but preventable medical errors that pervade our health care system …'

Immunization and screening

Immunization and health screening are effective ways of reducing illness in a population. Screening programmes aim to identify signs of illness at an early stage when treatment is comparatively easy and cheap.

Many new vaccines have been developed in the last 60 years, and some once-common deadly diseases have become rare in more

Widespread vaccination

VIEWPOINT

To wipe out polio by vaccinating all children, health-care workers need to penetrate even the remotest areas:

'Nigeria and India are responsible for the vast majority of new global polio cases. In Nigeria, we now have an effective vaccine to use and we've seen the start of improvements in vaccine uptake. These last pockets of unvaccinated children now need to be reached to achieve elimination in Nigeria and this in turn will have a dramatic impact on the prospects of worldwide eradication.'

(Helen Jenkins, Imperial College, London, UK)

This baby is about to receive a protective vaccination at a clinic in Nigeria.

economically developed countries. Parents are encouraged to have their children vaccinated. Sometimes, extra pressure is exerted. Children may not be allowed to attend school unless they have the recommended vaccinations. Immunization programmes are only successful if enough people are vaccinated. If most of the population is vaccinated, a disease cannot gain a foothold in the community.

Screening programmes depend on cheap, easy tests for common complaints. These use technologies such as X-ray and microscopic examination of cells to identify cancers before they produce noticeable tumours or symptoms. The first vaccine to protect against cancer went into use in 2007. The vaccine is given to teenage girls to protect them against a virus that causes cervical cancer.

 PROS: IMMUNIZATION AND SCREENING

Vaccination programmes are especially important in less economically developed countries where treatment is not always readily available. Scientists hope that polio will be the next disease (after smallpox) to be wiped out by widespread vaccination. Health screening catches signs of disease early when the condition is easy to treat. This may mean that less aggressive treatment can be used.

 CONS: IMMUNIZATION AND SCREENING

Sometimes, anxiety about a vaccine can prevent people using it. In 1998, a scare in the UK about the safety of the MMR vaccine, which protects children against measles, mumps and rubella, led to many parents refusing it. The diseases soon emerged again in the population.

Widespread health screening for particular diseases is costly and inevitably involves testing many people who are healthy. It can cause anxiety, particularly when positive results are reported to patients in error, or when extra testing is needed. For both screening and immunization programmes, the uptake (people taking part) is never 100 percent. Often, the people who do not come forward are those most at risk.

Mass protection

Sometimes, governments take action to protect whole populations. Some countries add fluoride to drinking water, because fluoride helps to protect against tooth decay. Around two-thirds of the population of the United States have fluoridated drinking water, compared with only 10 percent of the UK population. In some countries fluoride is added to salt or milk. Similarly, in some countries calcium is added to white flour. The calcium that is naturally present in flour is removed during processing. Adding calcium after processing restores a mineral needed by the body to build healthy bones and teeth.

To prevent disease, many countries spray large areas with insecticides to kill disease-carrying insects. In parts of southern Europe, spraying is carried out to destroy insects that carry infections such as dengue fever

A United Nations worker sprays a chemical to kill insect larvae on the island of Car Nicobar off the coast of India. The insects reproduce in pools of stagnant water such as this one.

and chikungunya fever. In some areas prone to malaria, the chemical DDT is sprayed to kill mosquitoes. Global warming is likely to mean that insects carrying dangerous diseases will change or extend their range, and be found in areas where they are currently not a threat. Spraying will probably increase in the next few years.

 PROS: MASS PROTECTION

Water fluoridation reduces the incidence of tooth decay, particularly in children. This saves money on later dental care, and gives individuals the benefit of longer-lasting, healthy teeth. The addition of calcium to flour helps to reduce the incidence of weak bones. Spraying pesticides to kill disease-carrying insects prevents people from catching diseases and reduces spending on health care.

 CONS: MASS PROTECTION

Mass programmes such as fluoridation and spraying take away personal choice. When fluoride is added to water, people have no control over whether they drink it or not. Too much fluoride can produce brown marks and small pits in the teeth. People cannot choose whether they and their property are exposed to insecticide spraying. DDT is a dangerous nerve toxin (poison) which is not permitted for purposes other than killing disease-carrying insects because it can have terrible side effects.

GM insects

Scientists hope to create genetically-modified insects that cannot carry diseases. These insects must be better able to survive than the corresponding natural insects so that they replace them in the ecosystem. If this plan works, insect-borne diseases could be reduced.

CHAPTER 9

Changing Lifestyles

To stay healthy, we all need to follow sensible regimes of hygiene, fitness and diet, and avoid overindulging in risky behaviour. There have been great advances in our understanding of many aspects of healthy living, resulting from scientific discoveries and research.

Hygiene and infection

Improvements in cleanliness and hygiene over the last 150 years have probably been the single most important factor in saving lives. The discovery that many illnesses are caused by microorganisms led to changing practices in hospitals and the development of new medicines. Today, hospitals try to reduce the risk of infection through rigorous cleaning.

Despite these measures, the development of 'superbugs' such as methicillin-resistant *Staphylococcus aureus* (MRSA) and *Clostridium difficile* has become a major problem in recent years. These bacteria are resistant to most antibiotics, and are most dangerous to people whose immune systems are already weakened because of illness or surgery. MRSA and *C. difficile* are easily passed from one patient to another, for example, on

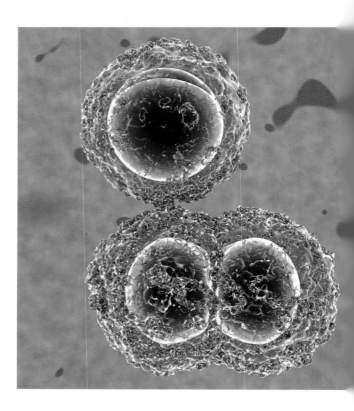

careworkers' hands. MRSA affected 278,000 hospital patients in the United States in 2005 – double the number infected in 1999. One way of tackling these infection rates is to 'deep clean' hospitals. This involves not just surface cleaning, but thorough cleaning of infrastructures such as heating and air-conditioning ducts.

Bacteria responsible for causing MRSA, a 'superbug' that commonly infects hospital patients.

PROS: HYGIENE

Generally-improved standards of cleanliness in communities have reduced life-threatening infections. The availability of strong, antibacterial cleaners for use in the home and elsewhere has reduced the chance of infection. Increased awareness of the risks of handling food with dirty hands, or allowing cross-contamination, has reduced the incidence of food poisoning.

 CONS: HYGIENE

Some scientists have suggested that the increasing cleanliness of many homes has led to a rise in the number of people with allergies and allergy-related symptoms, such as asthma. That is because the immune system develops by being confronted with threats and then combating them. Cleaner houses present fewer threats, and as a result people generally have weaker immune systems. The overuse of strong antibiotics has been blamed for the rise in hospital superbugs. The process of deep cleaning hospitals to try to control these superbugs has also been criticized. Deep cleaning is disruptive and expensive and some experts believe it will have little impact on infection rates. They say that money would be better spent on more effective day-to-day cleaning.

 **VIEWPOINT**

Simple measures

The most important method for preventing the spread of viral diseases is very simple and can be adopted by everyone:

'First and foremost to reduce virus transmission attention must be paid to hand-washing and then when this is satisfactory, focus on cleansing surfaces and equipment shared by others such as desks, tables, telephones and door knobs.'

(Professor John Oxford, Queen Mary's School of Medicine, London, UK)

Diet

To be healthy, people need to eat a balanced diet – a range of foods that provide the nutrients the body requires, such as fresh fruit and vegetables and sources of protein such as eggs, fish and lean meat. In some parts of the world, food scarcity means that people are undernourished. In other areas, food is plentiful, but some people still have a poor diet. People may eat too much of the wrong kind of food, such as fried foods and sugar, and become overweight or obese. Even overweight people may be malnourished if their food does not contain the nutrients they need.

The food industry has changed rapidly over the last 50 years. Factory farming and industrial processing have led to the mass production of cheap food. Genetic modification means animals or crops for food can be biologically altered, either to suit the needs of farmers and wholesalers, or to benefit consumers.

 PROS: FOOD INDUSTRY

Improvements in food production have made food more affordable. Technological innovations keep food usable for longer, which helps people to avoid food poisoning. In developing countries, genetically-modified food may help to provide people with the nutrients they are lacking in their restricted diets.

 CONS: FOOD INDUSTRY

The availability of cheap food has led to a huge increase in overweight and obese people. Obesity brings its own health risks, including heart disease and diabetes. Rates of diabetes and heart disease are increasing in many economically developed countries, even amongst children. Many scientific and technological developments in food production help producers but harm consumers. One example is the use of hydrogenated fats, which extend the shelf life of food but which have little or no nutritional benefit for most people. These fats increase the level of cholesterol in the blood and the likelihood of heart disease.

The rise in obesity

It is not just the amount of food that people eat which affects their health and can lead to obesity:

'We tend to assess food intake by the size of the portion, yet a fast food meal contains many more calories than a similar-sized portion of a healthy meal … Our bodies were never designed to cope with the very energy-dense foods consumed in the West and this is contributing to a major rise in obesity.'

(Professor Andrew Prentice, London School of Hygiene and Tropical Medicine, UK)

People often become overweight or obese as a result of an unhealthy diet.

Research and campaigns

Health education plays an important role in the improvement of general health. The discovery that smoking damages health was first made in the 1950s, and campaigns to warn people of the risks have run since the 1960s. Research into the effects of alcohol on unborn babies has led to public warnings that pregnant women should not drink. The discovery of HIV/AIDs, and the fact that the virus is transmitted in body fluids, resulted in health education campaigns to promote safe sex and to inform people about unsafe practices that could put them at risk. Governments publicize the results of research into diet and healthy body weight, launching campaigns to promote healthy eating and exercise, and limiting alcohol intake.

Legislation relating to public health is often the result of scientific research. For example, research into smoking led to laws requiring health warnings be printed on the packaging of tobacco products. It is also illegal to sell tobacco products to people under a certain age, and in many countries smoking is now banned in public places.

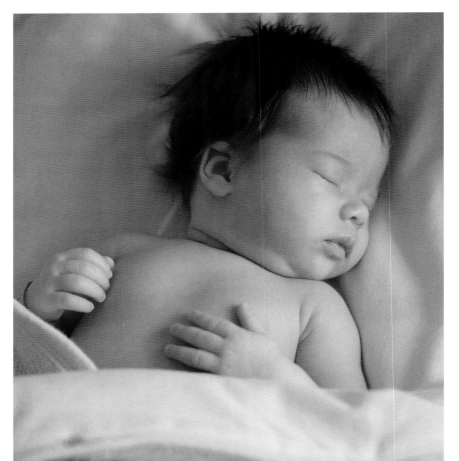

Research into Sudden Infant Death Syndrome (SIDS) led to public awareness campaigns to advise people about keeping their babies safe – for example, by putting babies down to sleep on their backs rather than on their fronts.

PROS: HEALTH EDUCATION

When new discoveries relating to healthy living are successfully communicated to a population, people can make their own choices and take responsibility for their own well-being. Improved health in the population leads to decreased spending on health care.

 CONS: HEALTH EDUCATION

Health education programmes do not always have the intended result. Sometimes, a campaign can seem to glamorize unhealthy behaviour. Health education alone may not be enough to change behaviour. People on low incomes may want to eat more healthily, but may only be able to afford cheaper processed or fast food. As scientific research progresses, our knowledge about healthy living is refined, and sometimes changes completely. People are often confused by what they see as conflicting or changing messages. Some may decide that no information seems reliable and stop paying attention.

VIEWPOINT

Too much information?

Everyone is exposed to an endless stream of information about health care and risks to health:

'A steady drumbeat of front-page controversies, surprises, and scandals over the past two years – ranging from Vioxx [a treatment for osteoarthritis withdrawn after worries that it increases the risk of heart attack and stroke], obesity-related mortality rates, estrogen, calcium, low-fat, stem cell research fraud, among others – threatens to seriously damage the credibility of health research, creating a risk that the public will turn away from public health pronouncements.'

(Jay Winsten, Frank Stanton Director of the Center for Health Communication, USA)

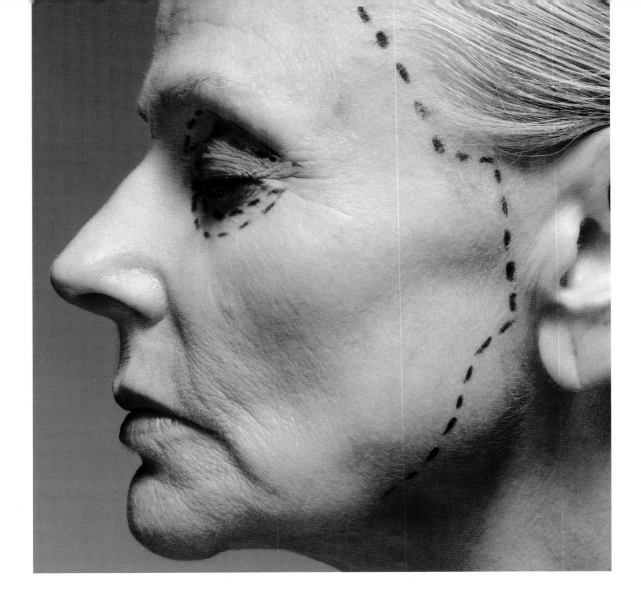

The perfect image

Increasing numbers of people are choosing plastic or cosmetic surgery in order to change their appearance to fit an ideal of what is beautiful. Plastic surgery began as reconstructive surgery, restoring the appearance of people damaged by injury or disease. The earliest known procedures, to rebuild noses removed as punishment, took place around 2,500 years ago in India. Today, much plastic surgery is carried out for purely cosmetic reasons. It includes procedures such as remodelling the face, anti-ageing treatments, removal of excess fat and reshaping of the breasts. A large number of teenagers, particularly in the United States, are having cosmetic surgery. As techniques have improved and surgery has become simpler, many people treat these operations like any other consumer purchase.

The dotted lines on this woman's face show where the cosmetic surgeon will cut when carrying out a facelift operation.

PROS: COSMETIC SURGERY

Many people feel better about themselves after changing their appearance. In the case of surgery to reduce obesity, people may be healthier afterwards and may adopt a healthier lifestyle to maintain their new look.

 CONS: COSMETIC SURGERY

Cosmetic surgery can mask deeper emotional or mental health issues. If a person opts for repeated treatments, there is often an underlying cause for their poor body image which should be investigated and treated. All surgical procedures can go wrong. Sometimes, people look much worse after surgery than before, and their health may be damaged. Implants that move around, go hard or burst can cause discomfort or even dangerous complications for some patients. The long-term effects of cosmetic surgery early in life are not yet fully known. Young people who have surgery before they have finished growing may be at particular risk of problems later on.

The 'perfect' body

VIEWPOINT

Teenagers, and particularly teenage girls, are especially influenced by popular images of beauty:

'Teenage girls are acutely aware of and influenced by the lengths adult women are prepared to risk their physical health in pursuit of a "perfect" body. Modern reality TV shows which focus on plastic surgery may seem laughable and grotesque to older people, but they have a worrying impact on teenage girls in the throes of puberty… while teenage girls are trying to establish a sense of their own value as humans, it is up to adults to teach them to be proud of their individuality.'

(Andrea Scherzer, psychotherapist, UK)

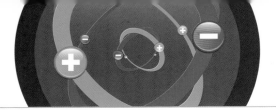

CHAPTER 10

Meeting New Challenges

The challenges facing medical science are constantly changing. New illnesses develop, old illnesses become resistant to established treatments, and changing lifestyles bring new health problems. Fifty years ago, HIV/AIDs had not been encountered, and the conditions caused by obesity were not widespread. Even success brings its own challenges. By freeing people from some of the diseases which once killed many, we have created an ageing population with new problems. The increase in heart disease and cancer is partly due to people surviving long enough to suffer from these conditions.

An ageing population puts pressure on health care services and governments. In some places, experimental systems that automate some aspects of geriatric (elderly) care are being used to reduce the burden on struggling systems without reducing the level of care that

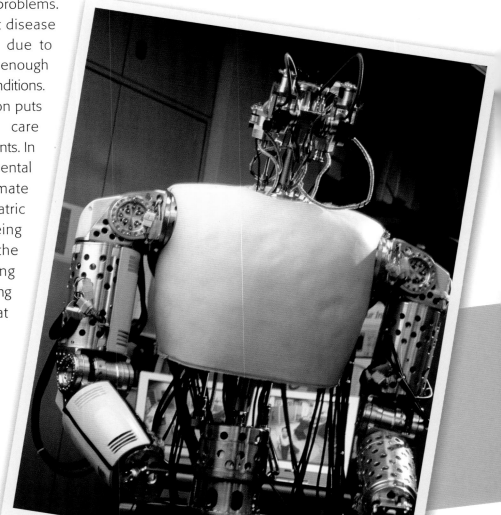

This humanoid robot has been developed in Japan. It has two cameras in the 'head', touch sensors and a microphone.

patients receive. For example, an elderly person's health, movements and interactions with other people can be monitored remotely using wireless networks. Such monitoring systems allow older people to live independently, while enabling their families and medical workers to make sure they are safe.

 PROS: AGEING POPULATIONS

Medical advances have meant that people are living longer than ever before in many parts of the world. Many of these people live healthy and independent lives. Many others keep chronic medical conditions under control with drugs or equipment such as a pacemaker.

 CONS: AGEING POPULATIONS

Not all elderly people are healthy and active. Many need constant care and attention. Conditions related to old age, such as stiffening or deteriorating joints, weak bones prone to fractures and mental problems such as dementia mean that some elderly people need operations, drugs and specialized help. The quality of life of some older people is very poor. An ageing population puts financial strain on health-care services and society as a whole. It is a challenge that societies around the world have to face.

The Pearl robot

In the United States and Japan, scientists are experimenting with robots that can carry out routine care for elderly people, either in their own homes or in care homes. Robots such as Pearl, developed in the United States, will eventually be able to lift and carry patients when necessary, respond to smell and help with simple self-care tasks. They can remind patients to take medication, or talk them through activities such as hand-washing if they need help.

GLOSSARY

aerate To add air to something.

AIDS (Acquired Immune Deficiency Syndrome)
A condition in which the body's immune system
stops working, causing patients to be vulnerable to
other diseases from which they eventually die.

Alzheimer's A condition in which brain function is
progressively lost. It usually starts with memory
problems and ends with loss of the senses and
control of the body, leading to death.

anaesthetic A substance that makes a person
unable to feel pain. Anaesthetics may act generally
or locally.

antibiotic A substance that kills or prevents the
growth of a microorganism, such as a bacterium.

antibody A type of cell produced by the body to
fight disease.

antimicrobial Describes a substance that kills or
prevents the growth of microbes, such as bacteria
or viruses.

antiseptic A substance applied to tissue to
prevent wounds becoming infected.

anti-rejection drug A medicine taken to prevent
the body fighting against and destroying new
tissue, such as a transplanted organ.

artery A blood vessel that carries blood from the
heart to the body.

autopsy An examination of a dead body to
determine the cause of death.

bacterium A very tiny, single-cell, living organism;
some bacteria cause disease.

bionic Combining biological and technological
parts or techniques.

bone marrow The tissue inside long bones where
new blood cells are produced.

carbolic acid (Also called phenol.) A poisonous
chemical that has antimicrobial properties.

cholera A dangerous and often deadly disease
spread through water contaminated with the
bacterium *Vibrio cholerae*. It causes extreme
diarrhoea and dehydration.

cholesterol A waxy chemical needed by the body
in small quantities. Too much cholesterol can lead
to blocked arteries and heart disease.

chromosome A structure found in cells. It is made
of DNA and protein and carries genetic
information.

computerized axial tomography (CAT) A scanner
that uses X-rays and a chemical contrast agent to
penetrate different tissues to different degrees.

deoxyribonucleic acid (DNA) A complex chemical
that codes genetic information through its
sequence of chemical components or building
blocks.

diabetes A condition in which the body is unable
to regulate the level of sugar in the blood because
of either a lack of the hormone insulin, or the
body's inability to recognize insulin.

electron microscope A microscope that produces
a clear image at a high magnification by firing a
beam of electrons at a sample.

embryo An unborn, partially developed organism.

GLOSSARY

ethical Relating to ideas of what is right and wrong.

fibre-optic cable A very thin glass or plastic fibre used to carry light.

fluoride A type of chemical that includes the element fluorine.

gene The basic unit of hereditary information, carried in DNA on a chromosome and providing the information needed for a single inherited trait.

gene therapy Treatment that involves making changes to genes or a person's genetic make-up.

genetically-modified (GM) Changed by adding or removing genes.

genetics The field of science that studies heredity (the way characteristics are passed from one generation of an organism to the next).

gynaecological Describes the branch of medicine that deals with the diagnosis and treatment of disorders affecting the female reproductive organs.

hepatitis A condition in which the liver is damaged and inflamed.

Human Immunodeficiency Virus (HIV) A virus that attacks the immune system and can lead to AIDS.

hydrogenated fat Fat that has been chemically changed by the addition of hydrogen. The process is used to make solid fats from liquid fats.

immune system The body's mechanism for fighting disease by producing antibodies.

immunization The process of giving someone a small quantity or deactivated version of a disease to make them immune to (able to withstand) the disease if they are exposed to it later.

in vitro fertilization (IVF) The fertilization of an egg outside the body.

insulin A hormone produced by the body that controls the level of glucose (sugar) in the blood.

invasive Going into or interfering with (the body).

kidney dialysis A process that performs the work of the kidneys in cleaning the blood, by routing the blood out of the body and through a dialysis machine.

laparoscopy Surgery that involves passing a lighted tube through a small cut to investigate, and sometimes operate on, the internal organs.

magnetic resonance imaging (MRI) A scanner that is used to get a picture of soft tissue inside the body, such as muscles and organs.

malaria A dangerous and often deadly disease carried by mosquitoes and causing bouts of extreme fever.

microbe A very small organism that can only be seen using a microscope (also microorganism).

microsurgery Surgery carried out on a very small scale, such as stitching small blood vessels or nerves, using tiny instruments and an operating microscope.

nutrient A chemical that is needed by an organism and must be taken from food or the environment.

GLOSSARY

obese Very overweight.

pacemaker A piece of equipment that is used to regulate the heartbeat.

Parkinson's disease A condition that causes progressive deterioration of the central nervous system, affecting the nerves and brain.

positron emission tomography (PET) A scanner that can be used to measure body functions, such as blood flow and oxygen use.

prosthetic An artificial aid that replaces a part of the body that has been lost.

protein A chemical with large molecules that makes up a major part of all organisms, from humans to bacteria and viruses.

radiation Energy emitted by chemical substances as they change from one state to another, losing particles or rays of energy.

retina The inner surface of the eyeball, with light-sensitive cells.

robotics The field of science that studies and develops robots.

sedate To put to sleep or subdue by lowering levels of awareness and response.

smallpox A dangerous viral disease characterized by a severe, painful rash, fever and back pain, often leading to blindness, brain damage or death.

stem cell An undifferentiated cell that can turn into one of many types of tissue cell (for example, bone, blood, muscle or skin).

sterilize To make completely clean, destroying bacteria and viruses.

telesurgery Surgery carried out remotely using computerized technology and robotic surgical tools.

thermal Relating to heat.

transfusion The introduction of blood into the body from an external source.

tumour A lump or swelling caused by excessive growth of cells. It can be benign (causing no harm) or malignant (dangerous and harmful).

ultrasound A very high-pitched sound that humans cannot hear.

umbilical cord The cord that connects the baby to the mother's placenta while it is in the womb, and which conveys nutrients to the growing baby.

vaccine A preparation given to a patient to build immunity to a disease, and which contains dead or deactivated viruses or bacteria.

virus A very tiny agent of infection that can grow only inside a cell.

xenotransplant The transplant of organs or tissues between different types of animal.

X-ray A form of electromagnetic radiation used to produce images of the inside of the body.

FURTHER INFORMATION

WEBSITES

Websites of major newspapers and news channels often cover breakthroughs in medicine:

http://topics.edition.cnn.com/topics/health_and_fitness

http://www.nytimes.com/pages/health/

http://www.washingtonpost.com/wp-dyn/content/health/wires/
(free registration required)

www.newscientist.com
The website of the magazine *New Scientist* often covers new breakthroughs and discoveries in medical science and technology.

http://news.bbc.co.uk/1/hi/health/default.stm
The BBC's updates on developments in health and medicine.

http://www.time.com/time/specials
Time magazine often covers new developments in medical science and technology.

BOOKS

From Cowpox to Antibiotics: Discovering Vaccines and Medicines
Carol Ballard, Heinemann (2006)

Cutting Edge Medicine: Fighting Infectious Diseases
Carol Ballard, Franklin Watts (2007)

Cutting Edge Medicine: Organ Transplantation
Carol Ballard, Franklin Watts (2007)

Science in the News: Cosmetic Surgery
Andrew Campbell, Franklin Watts (2008)

Science in the News: Organ Transplantation
Andrew Campbell, Franklin Watts (2008)

Why Science Matters: Finding Better Medicines
John Coad, Heinemann (2009)

Medicine's Brave New World
Margaret O. Hyde and John F. Setaro, Twenty-first Century Books (2001)

Cutting Edge Medicine: Machines in Medicine
Anne Rooney, Franklin Watts (2007)

The Cutting Edge: Medicine
Anne Rooney, Heinemann (2006)

Tomorrow's Science: Medicine Now
Anne Rooney, Chrysalis (2003)

Why Science Matters: Repairing and Replacing Organs
Andrew Solway, Heinemann (2009)

Science in the News: Genetics
Jenny Vaughan, Franklin Watts (2008)

Science in the News: Making New Life
Jenny Vaughan, Franklin Watts (2008)

INDEX

Page numbers in **BOLD** refer to illustrations and charts.

alcohol 54
Alzheimer's 27, 34
anaesthetics 5, 6
animal testing 18
antibiotic-resistant bacteria 23, 50
antibiotics 22-3, 50
  in farming 23
antiseptics 6
antivirals 22, 23, 25

bacteria 6, 16–17, 20, 21, 22, 23, 30, 50, **50**, 51
Barnard, Christiaan 38, **38**
Black Death 24
brain damage 11, 33

C. difficile 23, 50
calcium 48, 49, 55
cancer **18**, 18–19, 31, 32, 34, 47, 58
carbolic acid **4**, 6, 22
CAT scans 32, 33
chemotherapy 19
cholera 16, 21
chromosomes 26
clinical trials 18
computers 5, 6, 32, 34
  and health records 5, **44**, 44–5
  disease prediction 24
  in surgery 5, 6, 7
cord blood 27, 28
Crick, Francis 26
cystic fibrosis 28

Da Vinci robots 7, **7**
diabetes 30–31, 52
diet 50, 52–3, 54
Dinoire, Isabelle **43**
disease 5, 12, 16
  hereditary 28–9
  prevention 20–21, 46–9
  transmission 16
  treatments 17, 18–19, 22, 23, 27
DNA 26, 30

electron microscopes 16, **18**, **27**
embryos 27, 28, **29**
endoscopy **36**, 36–7

fast food 53, **53**, 55
Fleming, Alexander 22, **22**
fluoridation 48–9
Franklin, Rosalind 26

gene therapy 31
genes 5, 21, 26–31
genetic engineering 21, 30–31, 39, 49, 52
genetic screening 28–9, 31
geriatric care 58-9

health education 54–5
health screening 46–7
heart-lung machines 8, **8**, 38
hepatitis 21, 41
HIV/AIDS 41, 54, 58
Human Genome Project 26
Huntington's chorea 28
hydrogenated fats 52
hygiene 50-1

implants 12–13, 33, 37, 57
  heart pacemakers 12–13, 33
  retinal 13
influenza 17, 21, 24
  avian **24**, 24–5
  Spanish flu 17, **17**, 24
insulin 30, **30**, 31
intensive-care units (ICUs) 10–11
internet 5, 6, 44, 45
IVF 28, 29, **29**

Jenner, Edward 20

laparoscopy 8, 37
limbs
  artificial (prosthetic) 12, 14–15, **15**
  biohybrid 14
Lister, Joseph **4**, 6, 22

measles 20, 47
Mendel, Gregor 26
MRI scans 32, 33, **33**
MRSA 23, 50, **50**

nanoparticles 19
neurotechnology 14
Nightingale, Florence 10, **10**

obesity 52–3, 55, 57, 58

pandemics 17, 24–5
Parkinson's disease 27
Pasteur, Louis 5, 16, 22
pasteurization 22

PET scans 34
premature (preterm) babies 10, 11
prophylactics 20–21

radiotherapy 19
replacement joints **12**, 12–13,
robotics 4, 5, 6, 7, **7**, 14, **58**, 58–9,
Roentgen, Wilhelm 32

Schiavo, Terry 11
smallpox 17, 20, 21, 47
smoking 54
Snow, John 16
spraying 48, 48–9
special-care baby units 11
stem cells 26–8, **27**, 41
sterilization **4**, 6, 22
stethoscopes 5
surgery **4**, 5, 6–9, **7**, 12, 13, 22, 23, **36**, 36–7, 38–43, 50
  cosmetic (plastic) **56**, 56–7
  heart 8–9

telesurgery 5, 6, 7, **7**
thermal imaging 35
thermometers 5
transplants 38–43
  arm 42
  blood 40–41
  bone marrow **40**, 40–41
  face 42, 43, **43**
  hand 42
  heart 38, **38**
  heart-lung 38–9
  kidney 40
  liver 40, 41
  living donors 40–41

ultrasound **34**, 35

vaccinations **20**, 20–21, 24, 31, **46**, 46–7
  MMR vaccine 47
viruses **16**, 16–17, 20, 21, 22, 24, 25, 47, 51, 54

Watson, James 26

xenotransplants 39
X-rays **12**, 32, 37, **38**, 47